contemporary TV THEMES

contents

ISBN 0-634-06694-3

HAL•LEONARD®
CORPORATION
7777 W. BLUEMOUND RD. P.O. BOX 13819 MILWAUKEE, WI 53213

Visit Hal Leonard Online at
www.halleonard.com

AMERICAN IDOL THEME
from AMERICAN IDOL

Words and Music by JULIAN GINGELL,
BARRY STONE and CATHY DENNIS

Moderately fast

8vb throughout

Original key: F♯ major. This edition has been transposed down one half-step to be more playable.

BEANS AND CORNBREAD
from DINNER & A MOVIE

Words and Music by FREDDIE CLARK
and FLEECIE MOORE

mor-row night. ____ I'll be read-y, I'll ____ be ____ read-y to-mor-row night." ____ That's what Beans ____ said to

Corn-bread: "I'll ____ be ____ read-y to-mor-row night." ____ Beans ____ told Corn-bread, "You ain't straight. You bet-ter wake up ____ or I'll

G6

gash your gate. Been in this pot since half ___ past two,

swell-in' and puff-in' and al - most due." "I'll ___ be

read - y, I'll ___ be read - y to - mor - row night. ___ (Beans ___

___ and Corn - bread, Beans ___ and Corn - bread

Lead vocal (Spoken): That's what Beans told Cornbread.

let me go." Corn - bread said, "I'll lay ___ you low. ___ I'm ___

___ gon - na fight ___ you, you so - and - so." "Meet me ___ on the

cor - ner. Meet me on the cor - ner to - mor - row night." ("Meet

me ___ on the cor - ner. Meet me on the cor - ner to -

Spoken: (See spoken lyrics I)

1, 2
3

mor - row night. Meet mor - row night.") Beans __ hit Corn - bread

on the head, but Corn - bread said, "I'm al -

- most dead." Beans __ told Corn - bread, "Get up, man; you

know that we go hand in hand." Beans and

Corn - bread, Beans ___ and Corn - bread hand in hand. (Beans ___

___ and Corn - bread, Beans ___ and Corn - bread

Spoken: (See spoken lyric II)

1, 2 | **3**

hand in hand.) (Beans ___ hand in hand.) (Beans.) ___

Play 15 times

Spoken: (See spoken lyrics III)

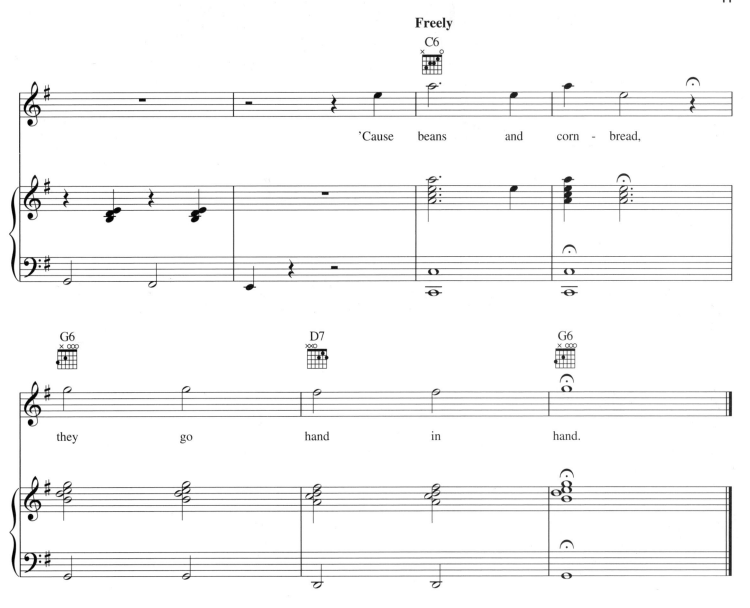

Freely

'Cause beans and corn-bread,

they go hand in hand.

Spoken lyrics I:

That's what Beans said to Cornbread:
"You're so bad, you always wanna fight.
Meet y'all at the corner tomorrow night,
and I'm gonna beat the hell out ya.
Ooh, ooh, ooh, ooh, ooh, ooh, on the
corner tomorrow night.

Spoken lyrics II:

That's what Beans said to Cornbread:
"We should stick together hand in hand.
We should hang out together like
weiners and sauerkraut. We should
stick together like hot dogs and mustard.
We should get up every morning and
hang out together like sisters and brothers.

Spoken lyrics III:

Every Saturday night we should hang out
like chitlins and potato salad, (Yeah!)
like strawberry and shortcake, (Yeah!)
like corned beef and cabbage, (Yeah!)
like liver and onions, (Yeah!)
like red beans and rice, (Yeah!)
like bagel and lox, (Yeah!)
like sour cream and blintz, (Yeah!)
like bread and butter, (Yeah!)
like hotcakes and molasses." (Yeah!)
Beans told Cornbread, "It makes no
difference what you think about me, (Yeah!)
but it makes a whole lot of difference
what I think about you. (Yeah!)
We should hang out together
like hotcakes and molasses." (Yeah!)
That's what Beans said to Cornbread.

BEVERLY HILLS 90210
(Main Theme)
from the Television Series BEVERLY HILLS 90210

By JOHN E. DAVIS

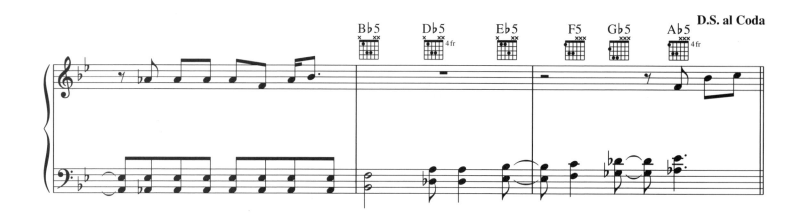

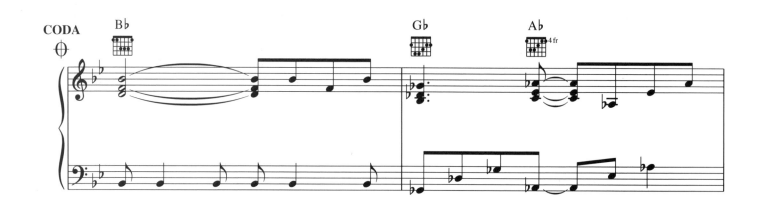

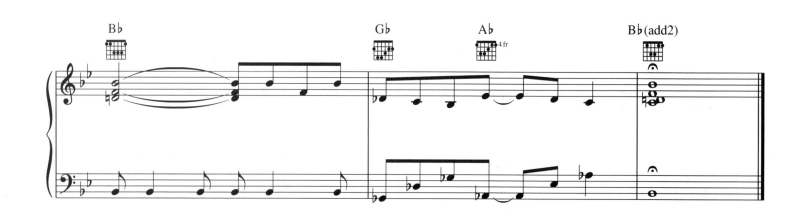

DORA THE EXPLORER THEME SONG

from DORA THE EXPLORER

Words and Music by JOSH SITRON,
BILLY STRAUS and SARAH DURKEE

Bright Salsa feel

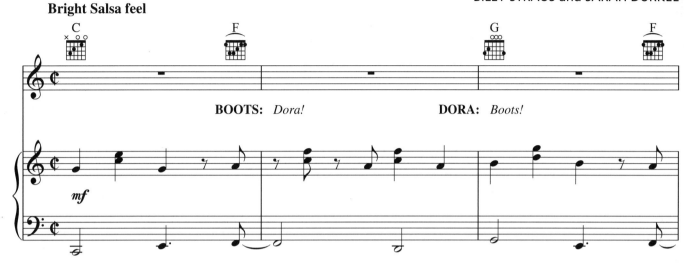

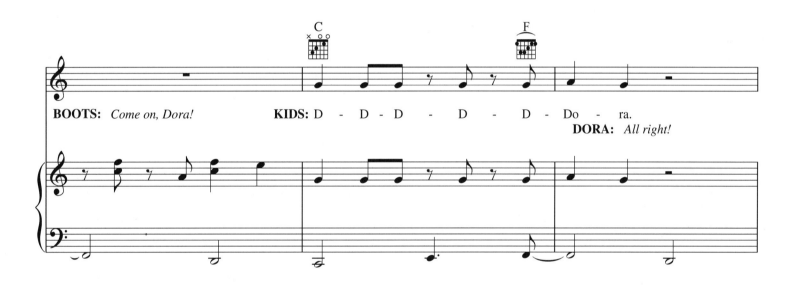

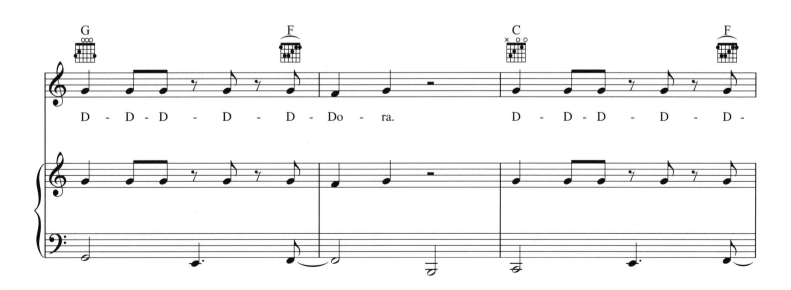

CLEVELAND ROCKS
Theme from THE DREW CAREY SHOW

Words and Music by
IAN HUNTER

CLOSER TO FREE

from PARTY OF FIVE

Words and Music by SAM LLANAS
and KURT NEUMANN

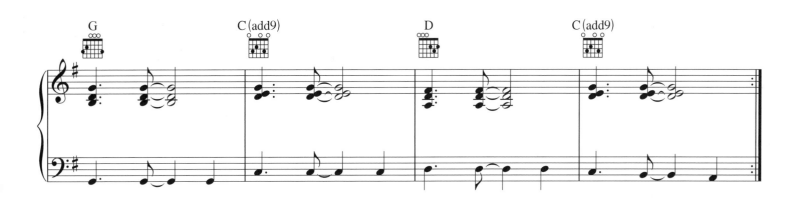

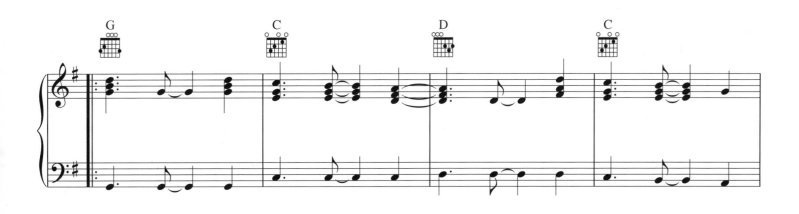

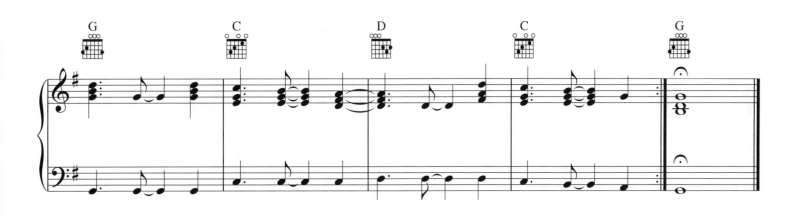

ENTERPRISE THEME
(Where My Heart Will Take Me)
from the Paramount T.V. Series STAR TREK: ENTERPRISE

Words and Music by
DIANE WARREN

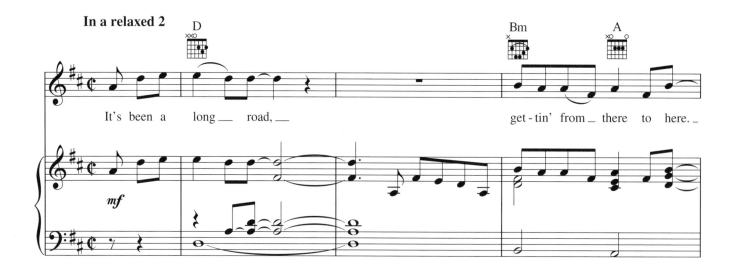

It's been a long road, gettin' from there to here.

It's been a long time, but my time is fin-'lly near.

But I will see my dream come a-live at last; I will touch the sky.

EMPIRE IN MY MIND

from THE GUARDIAN

Words and Music by
JAKOB DYLAN

Moderately slow, steady

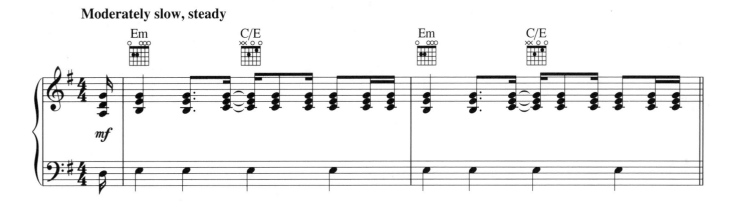

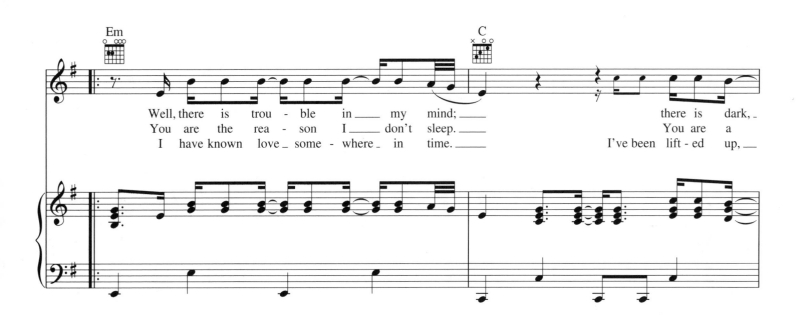

Well, there is trou-ble in ___ my mind; ___ there is dark, ___
You are the rea-son I ___ don't sleep. ___ You are a
I have known love ___ some-where in time. ___ I've been lift-ed up, ___

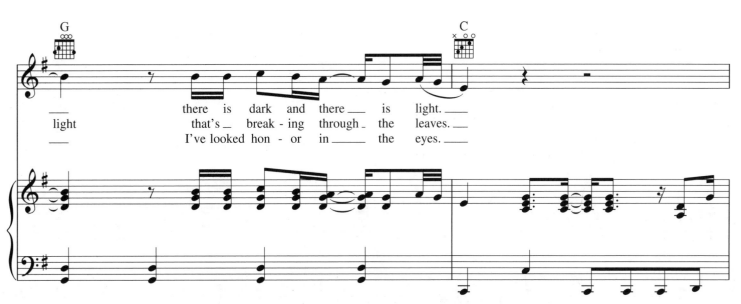

___ light there is dark and there ___ is light. ___
light that's ___ break-ing through ___ the leaves. ___
___ I've looked hon-or in ___ the eyes.

in the em - pire ___ in my mind. ___

There is no dis - tance that I don't see. __

I do have a will, ___ no lim - it to ___ my reach. __

I wish I would, _ I wish I might __

ENTERTAINMENT TONIGHT
Theme from the Paramount Television Show

Music by MICHAEL MARK

Moderately fast

THE NANNY NAMED FRAN

from the TV series THE NANNY

Words and Music by
ANN HAMPTON CALLAWAY

THEME FROM "FRASIER"

from the Paramount Television Series FRASIER

Words by DARRYL PHINNESSEE
Music by BRUCE MILLER

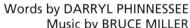

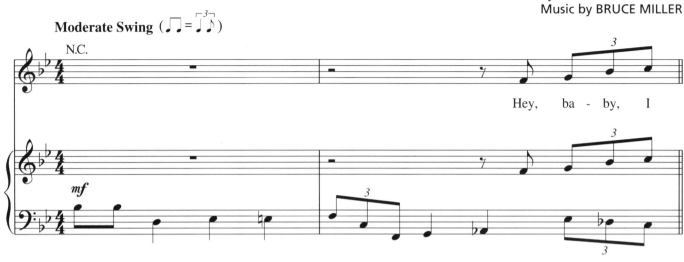

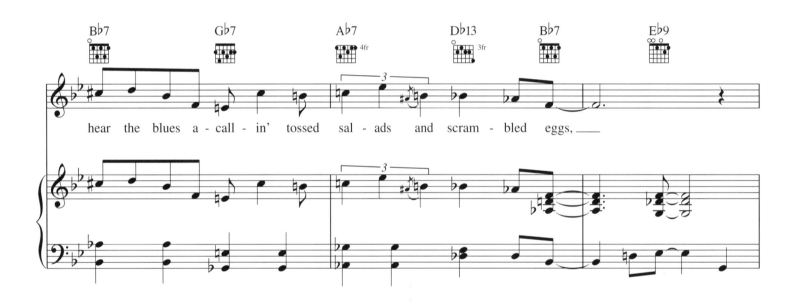

HOME IMPROVEMENT
Theme from the TV Series

Music by DAN FOLIART

I DON'T WANT TO WAIT

featured in DAWSON'S CREEK

Words and Music by
PAULA COLE

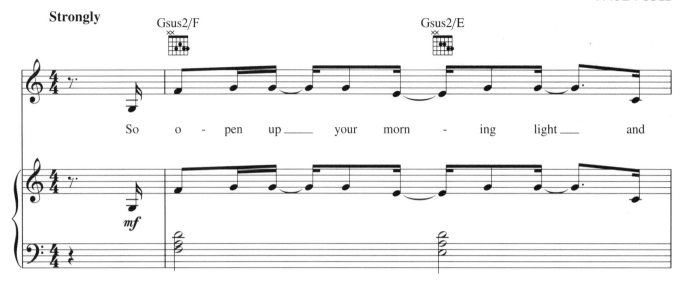

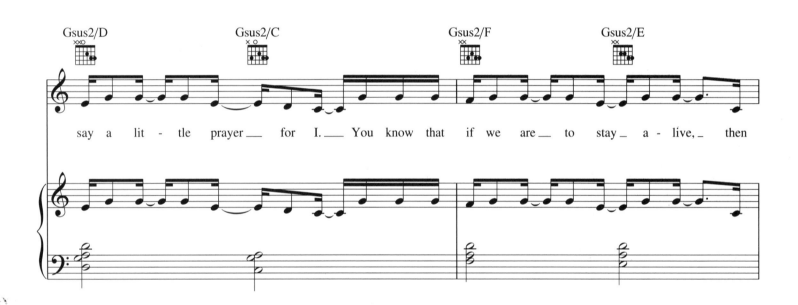

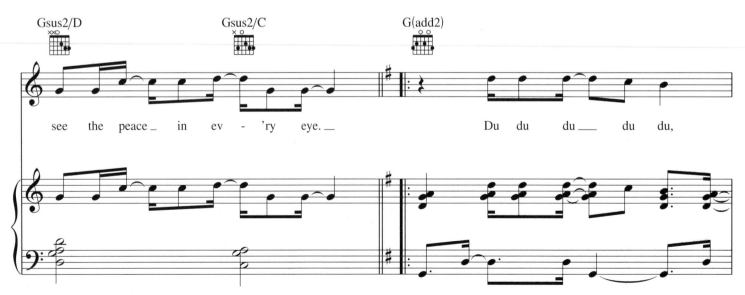

MELROSE PLACE THEME
from the Television Series MELROSE PLACE

By TIM TRUMAN

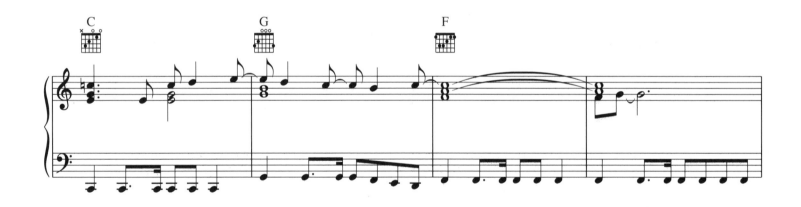

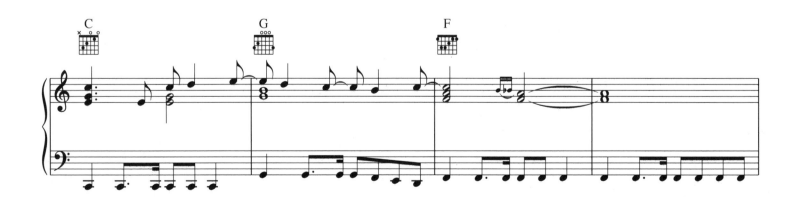

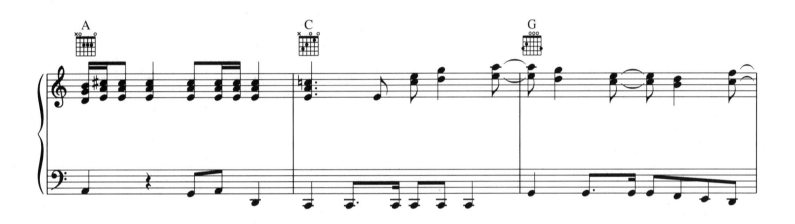

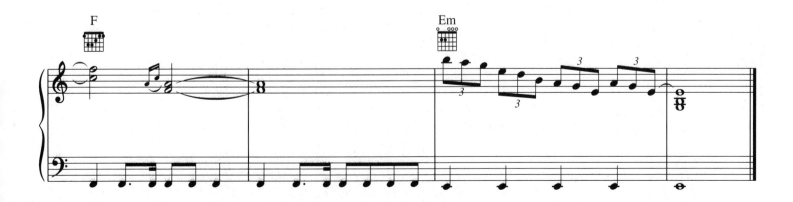

NEXT YEAR

from ED

Words and Music by DAVE GROHL,
NATE MENDEL and TAYLOR HAWKINS

Moderately

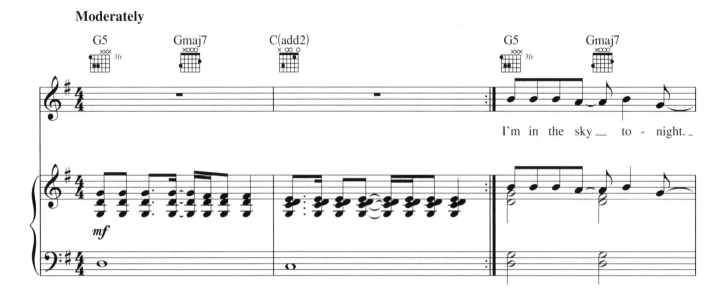

I'm in the sky __ to - night. __

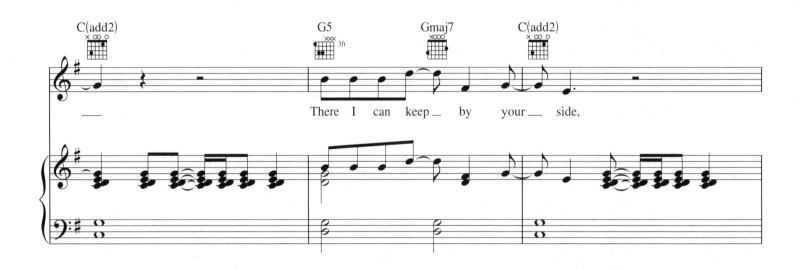

There I can keep __ by your __ side,

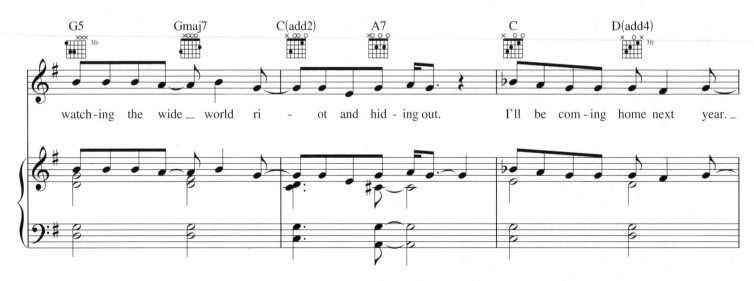

watch-ing the wide __ world ri - ot and hid-ing out. I'll be com-ing home next year. __

D.S. al Coda

WOKE UP THIS MORNING

from THE SOPRANOS

Words and Music by JAKE BLACK,
CHESTER BURNETT, SIMON EDWARDS,
PIER MARSH and ROBERT SPRAGG

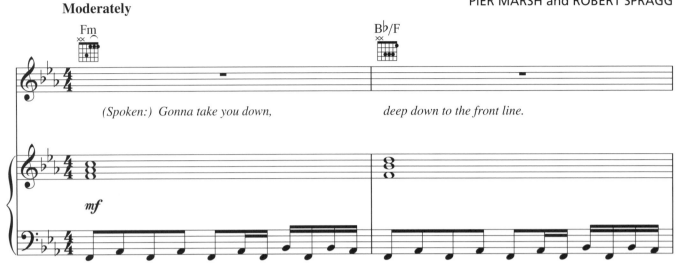

(Spoken:) Gonna take you down,   deep down to the front line.

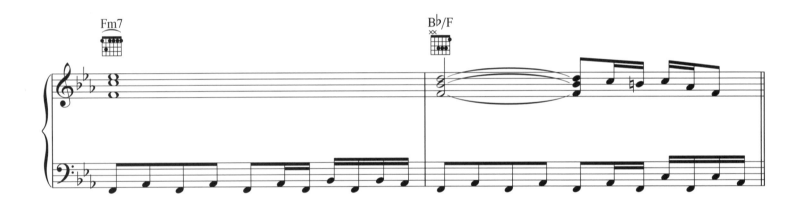

*You woke up this morn - ing, __ got your - self a gun. __
woke up this morn - ing, __ all that love had gone. __
woke up this morn - ing, __ the world turned up - side down, __ Lord __ a - bove.

*Lead vocal sung two octaves below written pitch.

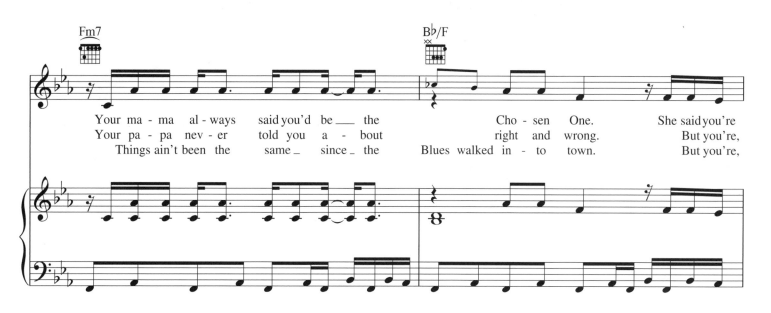

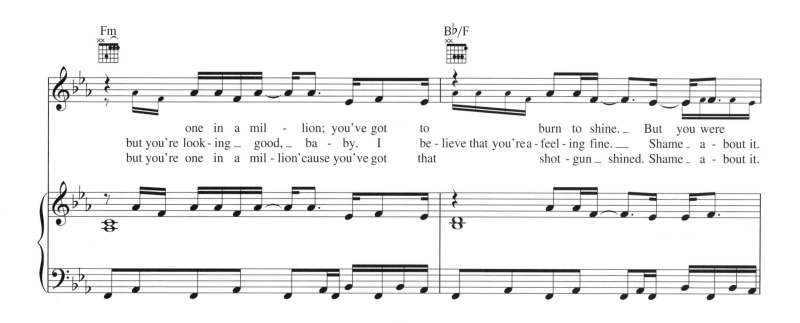

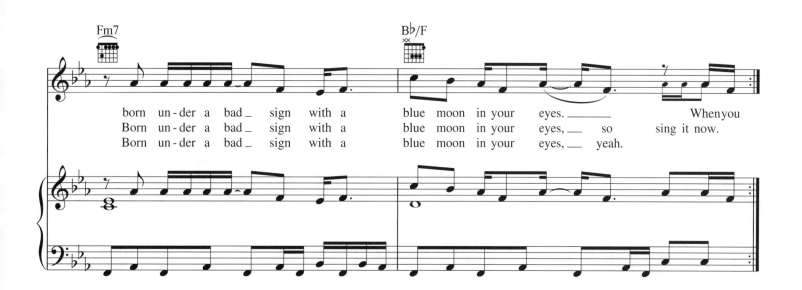

Rap Lyrics

When you woke up this morning, everything was gone.
By half past ten your head was going ding-dong,
Ringing like a bell from your head down to your toes,
Like a voice trying to tell you there's something you should know.

Last night you was flying, but today you're so low.
Ain't it times like these makes you wonder if you'll ever know
The meaning of things as they appear to the others:
Wives, husbands, mothers, fathers, sisters and brothers?

Don't you wish you didn't function, don't you wish you never think
Beyond the next paycheck and the next little drink?
Well you do, so make up your mind to go on, 'cause when you
Woke up this morning, everything you had was gone.

REGIS AND KATHIE LEE THEME

from LIVE! WITH REGIS AND KATHIE LEE

By SHELTON PALMER

7TH HEAVEN MAIN THEME

Theme from the Spelling Television Series 7TH HEAVEN

Words and Music by STEVE PLUNKETT,
JACK TEMPCHIN and JOHNNY RIVERS

Moderately fast

Sev - enth Heav - en, when I see their __ hap - py fac - es smil - in' back __ at me. __ Sev - enth Heav - en, I know there's no __ great - er feel - in' than the love of __ fam - i - ly. __ Where can you

SPONGEBOB SQUAREPANTS THEME SONG

from SPONGEBOB SQUAREPANTS

Words and Music by MARK HARRISON,
BLAISE SMITH, STEVE HILLENBURG
and DEREK DRYMON

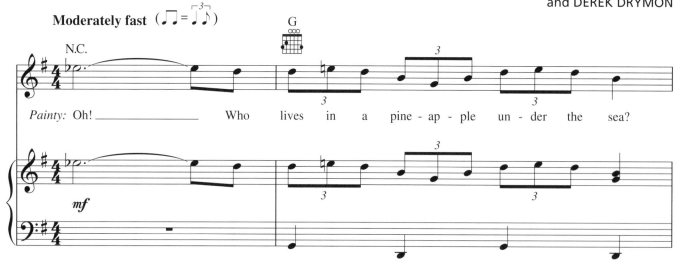

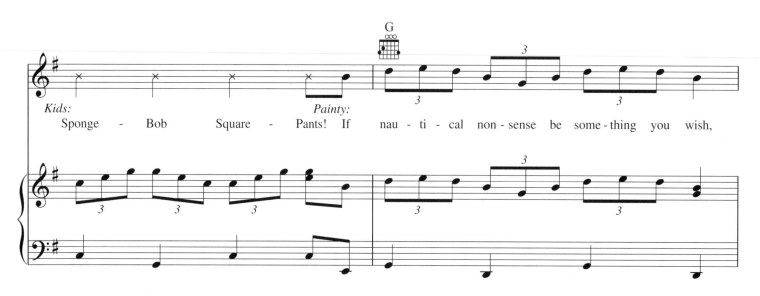

THE BEST EVER COLLECTION

ARRANGED FOR PIANO, VOICE AND GUITAR

150 of the Most Beautiful Songs Ever
150 ballads: Bewitched • (They Long to Be) Close to You • How Deep Is Your Love • I'll Be Seeing You • Unchained Melody • Yesterday • Young at Heart • more.
00360735..............................$22.95

Best Acoustic Rock Songs Ever
65 acoustic hits: Dust in the Wind • Fast Car • I Will Remember You • Landslide • Leaving on a Jet Plane • Maggie May • Tears in Heaven • Yesterday • more.
00310984..............................$19.95

Best Big Band Songs Ever
Over 60 big band hits: Boogie Woogie Bugle Boy • Don't Get Around Much Anymore • In the Mood • Moonglow • Sentimental Journey • Who's Sorry Now • more.
00359129..............................$16.95

Best Broadway Songs Ever
Over 70 songs in all! Includes: All I Ask of You • Bess, You Is My Woman • Climb Ev'ry Mountain • Comedy Tonight • If I Were a Rich Man • Ol' Man River • more!
00309155..............................$20.95

Best Children's Songs Ever
Over 100 songs: Bingo • Eensy Weensy Spider • The Farmer in the Dell • On Top of Spaghetti • Puff the Magic Dragon • Twinkle, Twinkle Little Star • and more.
00310360 (Easy Piano)..............................$19.95

Best Christmas Songs Ever
More than 60 holiday favorites: Frosty the Snow Man • A Holly Jolly Christmas • I'll Be Home for Christmas • Rudolph, The Red-Nosed Reindeer • Silver Bells • more.
00359130..............................$19.95

Best Classic Rock Songs Ever
Over 60 hits: American Woman • Bang a Gong • Cold As Ice • Heartache Tonight • Rock and Roll All Nite • Smoke on the Water • Wonderful Tonight • and more.
00310800..............................$18.95

Best Classical Music Ever
Over 80 of classical favorites: Ave Maria • Canon in D • Eine Kleine Nachtmusik • Für Elise • Lacrymosa • Ode to Joy • William Tell Overture • and many more.
00310674..............................$19.95

Best Contemporary Christian Songs Ever
Over 70 favorites, including: Awesome God • El Shaddai • Friends • Jesus Freak • People Need the Lord • Place in This World • Serve the Lord • Thy Word • more.
00310558..............................$19.95

Best Country Songs Ever
78 classic country hits: Always on My Mind • Crazy • Daddy Sang Bass • Forever and Ever, Amen • God Bless the U.S.A. • I Fall to Pieces • Through the Years • more.
00359135..............................$17.95

Best Early Rock N Roll Songs Ever
Over 70 songs, including: Book of Love • Crying • Do Wah Diddy Diddy • Louie, Louie • Peggy Sue • Shout • Splish Splash • Stand By Me • Tequila • and more.
00310816..............................$17.95

Best Easy Listening Songs Ever
75 mellow favorites: (They Long to Be) Close to You • Every Breath You Take • How Am I Supposed to Live Without You • Unchained Melody • more.
00359193..............................$18.95

Best Gospel Songs Ever
80 gospel songs: Amazing Grace • Daddy Sang Bass • How Great Thou Art • I'll Fly Away • Just a Closer Walk with Thee • The Old Rugged Cross • more.
00310503..............................$19.95

Best Hymns Ever
118 hymns: Abide with Me • Every Time I Feel the Spirit • He Leadeth Me • I Love to Tell the Story • Were You There? • When I Survey the Wondrous Cross • and more.
00310774..............................$17.95

Best Jazz Standards Ever
77 jazz hits: April in Paris • Don't Get Around Much Anymore • Love Is Here to Stay • Misty • Satin Doll • Unforgettable • When I Fall in Love • and more.
00311641..............................$19.95

More of the Best Jazz Standards Ever
74 beloved jazz hits: Ain't Misbehavin' • Blue Skies • Come Fly with Me • Honeysuckle Rose • The Lady Is a Tramp • Moon River • My Funny Valentine • and more.
00311023..............................$19.95

Best Latin Songs Ever
67 songs: Besame Mucho (Kiss Me Much) • The Girl from Ipanema • Malaguena • Slightly Out of Tune (Desafinado) • Summer Samba (So Nice) • and more.
00310355..............................$19.95

Best Love Songs Ever
65 favorite love songs, including: Endless Love • Here and Now • Love Takes Time • Misty • My Funny Valentine • So in Love • You Needed Me • Your Song.
00359198..............................$19.95

Best Movie Songs Ever
74 songs from the movies: Almost Paradise • Chariots of Fire • My Heart Will Go On • Take My Breath Away • Unchained Melody • You'll Be in My Heart • more.
00310063..............................$19.95

Best R&B Songs Ever
66 songs, including: Baby Love • Endless Love • Here and Now • I Will Survive • Saving All My Love for You • Stand By Me • What's Going On • and more.
00310184..............................$19.95

Best Rock Songs Ever
Over 60 songs: All Shook Up • Blue Suede Shoes • Born to Be Wild • Every Breath You Take • Free Bird • Hey Jude • We Got the Beat • Wild Thing • more!
00490424..............................$18.95

Best Songs Ever
Over 70 must-own classics: Edelweiss • Love Me Tender • Memory • My Funny Valentine • Tears in Heaven • Unforgettable • A Whole New World • and more.
00359224..............................$22.95

More of the Best Songs Ever
79 more favorites: April in Paris • Candle in the Wind • Endless Love • Misty • My Blue Heaven • My Heart Will Go On • Stella by Starlight • Witchcraft • more.
00310437..............................$19.95

Best Standards Ever, Vol. 1 (A-L)
72 beautiful ballads, including: All the Things You Are • Bewitched • God Bless' the Child • I've Got You Under My Skin • The Lady Is a Tramp • more.
00359231..............................$16.95

Best Standards Ever, Vol. 2 (M-Z)
72 songs: Makin' Whoopee • Misty • My Funny Valentine • People Will Say We're in Love • Smoke Gets in Your Eyes • Strangers in the Night • Tuxedo Junction • more.
00359232..............................$16.95

More of the Best Standards Ever, Vol. 1 (A-L)
76 all-time favorites: Ain't Misbehavin' • Always • Autumn in New York • Desafinado • Fever • Fly Me to the Moon • Georgia on My Mind • and more.
00310813..............................$17.95

More of the Best Standards Ever, Vol. 2 (M-Z)
75 more stunning standards: Mona Lisa • Mood Indigo • Moon River • Norwegian Wood • Route 66 • Sentimental Journey • Stella by Starlight • What'll I Do? • and more.
00310814..............................$17.95

Best Torch Songs Ever
70 sad and sultry favorites: All by Myself • Crazy • Fever • I Will Remember You • Misty • Stormy Weather (Keeps Rainin' All the Time) • Unchained Melody • and more.
00311027..............................$19.95

Best TV Songs Ever
Over 50 fun and catchy theme songs: The Addams Family • The Brady Bunch • Happy Days • Mission: Impossible • Where Everybody Knows Your Name • and more!
00311048..............................$17.95

FOR MORE INFORMATION, SEE YOUR LOCAL MUSIC DEALER, OR WRITE TO:

HAL•LEONARD™ CORPORATION

7777 W. BLUEMOUND RD. P.O. BOX 13819 MILWAUKEE, WI 53213

Visit us on-line for complete songlists at
www.halleonard.com